by Iain Gray

PUBLISHING

WRITING *to* REMEMBER

79 Main Street, Newtongrange,
Midlothian EH22 4NA
Tel: 0131 344 0414   Fax: 0845 075 6085
E-mail: info@lang-syne.co.uk
www.langsyneshop.co.uk

Design by Dorothy Meikle
Printed by Printwell Ltd
© Lang Syne Publishers Ltd 2019

All rights reserved. No part of this publication may be reproduced, stored
or introduced into a retrieval system, or transmitted in any form or by any
means (electronic, mechanical, photocopying, recording or otherwise) without
the prior written permission of Lang Syne Publishers Ltd.

ISBN 978-1-85217-641-9

Hall

MOTTO:
Live so that you may live.

CREST:
The head of the hunting hound known as a Talbot.

NAME variations include:
Hal
Hale
Haugh
Ha
Halle
Haul

Chapter one:

The origins of popular surnames

by George Forbes and Iain Gray

***If you don't know where you came from, you won't know where you're going* is a frequently quoted observation and one that has a particular resonance today when there has been a marked upsurge in interest in genealogy, with increasing numbers of people curious to trace their family roots.**

Main sources for genealogical research include census returns and official records of births, marriages and deaths – and the key to unlocking the detail they contain is obviously a family surname, one that has been 'inherited' and passed from generation to generation.

No matter our station in life, we all have a surname – but it was not until about the middle of the fourteenth century that the practice of being identified by a particular surname became commonly established throughout the British Isles.

Previous to this, it was normal for a person to be identified through the use of only a forename.

But as population gradually increased and there were many more people with the same forename, surnames were adopted to distinguish one person, or community, from another.

Many common English surnames are patronymic in origin, meaning they stem from the forename of one's father – with 'Johnson,' for example, indicating 'son of John.'

It was the Normans, in the wake of their eleventh century conquest of Anglo-Saxon England, a pivotal moment in the nation's history, who first brought surnames into usage – although it was a gradual process.

For the Normans, these were names initially based on the title of their estates, local villages and chateaux in France to distinguish and identify these landholdings.

Such grand descriptions also helped enhance the prestige of these warlords and generally glorify their lofty positions high above the humble serfs slaving away below in the pecking order who had only single names, often with Biblical connotations as in Pierre and Jacques.

The only descriptive distinctions among the peasantry concerned their occupations, like 'Pierre the swineherd' or 'Jacques the ferryman.'

Roots of surnames that came into usage in England not only included Norman-French, but also Old French, Old Norse, Old English, Middle English, German, Latin, Greek, Hebrew and the Gaelic languages of the Celts.

The Normans themselves were originally Vikings, or 'Northmen', who raided, colonised and eventually settled down around the French coastline.

The had sailed up the Seine in their longboats in 900AD under their ferocious leader Rollo and ruled the roost in north eastern France before sailing over to conquer England in 1066 under Duke William of Normandy – better known to posterity as William the Conqueror, or King William I of England.

Granted lands in the newly-conquered England, some of their descendants later acquired territories in Wales, Scotland and Ireland – taking not only their own surnames, but also the practice of adopting a surname, with them.

But it was in England where Norman rule and custom first impacted, particularly in relation to the adoption of surnames.

This is reflected in the famous *Domesday Book*, a massive survey of much of England and Wales, ordered by William I, to determine who owned what, what it was worth and therefore how much they were liable to pay in taxes to the voracious Royal Exchequer.

Completed in 1086 and now held in the National Archives in Kew, London, 'Domesday' was an Old English word meaning 'Day of Judgement.'

This was because, in the words of one contemporary chronicler, "its decisions, like those of the Last Judgement, are unalterable."

It had been a requirement of all those English landholders – from the richest to the poorest – that they identify themselves for the purposes of the survey and for future reference by means of a surname.

This is why the *Domesday Book*, although written in Latin as was the practice for several centuries with both civic and ecclesiastical records, is an invaluable source for the early appearance of a wide range of English surnames.

Several of these names were coined in connection with occupations.

These include Baker and Smith, while Cooks, Chamberlains, Constables and Porters were to be found carrying out duties in large medieval households.

The church's influence can be found in names such as Bishop, Friar and Monk while the popular name of Bennett derives from the late fifth to mid-sixth century Saint Benedict, founder of the Benedictine order of monks.

The early medical profession is represented by Barber, while businessmen produced names that include Merchant and Sellers.

Down at the village watermill, the names that cropped up included Millar/Miller, Walker and Fuller, while other self-explanatory trades included Cooper, Tailor, Mason and Wright.

Even the scenery was utilised as in Moor, Hill, Wood and Forrest – while the hunt and the chase supplied names that include Hunter, Falconer, Fowler and Fox.

Colours are also a source of popular surnames, as in Black, Brown, Gray/Grey, Green and White, and would have denoted the colour of the clothing the person habitually wore or, apart from the obvious exception of 'Green', one's hair colouring or even complexion.

The surname Red developed into Reid, while

Blue was rare and no-one wanted to be associated with yellow.

Rather self-important individuals took surnames that include Goodman and Wiseman, while physical attributes crept into surnames such as Small and Little.

Many families proudly boast the heraldic device known as a Coat of Arms, as featured on our front cover.

The central motif of the Coat of Arms would originally have been what was borne on the shield of a warrior to distinguish himself from others on the battlefield.

Not featured on the Coat of Arms, but highlighted on page three, is the family motto and related crest – with the latter frequently different from the central motif.

Adding further variety to the rich cultural heritage that is represented by surnames is the appearance in recent times in lists of the 100 most common names found in England of ones that include Khan, Patel and Singh – names that have proud roots in the vast sub-continent of India.

Echoes of a far distant past can still be found in our surnames and they can be borne with pride in commemoration of our forebears.

Chapter two:

Norman roots

A name derived from the Old French 'halle', meaning a large manorial hall, 'Hall' is both an occupational and a locational surname originally denoting someone who worked or lived in or near such a hall.

In medieval times, the 'hall' in question would have been the home of anyone wealthy enough to employ live-in servants, such as a steward to handle domestic and business accounts.

Yet another possible derivation is from the Anglo-Saxon 'halla' or the Norse 'holl', both of which indicate a large house.

But it was undoubtedly, in common with many other surnames found in England today, first popularised in the wake of the pivotal event in history that was the Norman Conquest of 1066.

By this date, England had become a nation with several powerful competitors to the throne.

In what were extremely complex family, political and military machinations, the monarch was

Harold II, who had succeeded to the throne following the death of Edward the Confessor.

But his right to the throne was contested by two powerful competitors – his brother-in-law King Harold Hardrada of Norway, in alliance with Tostig, Harold II's brother, and Duke William II of Normandy.

In what has become known as The Year of Three Battles, Hardrada invaded England and gained victory over the English king on September 20 at the battle of Fulford, in Yorkshire.

Five days later, however, Harold II decisively defeated his brother-in-law and brother at the battle of Stamford Bridge.

But he had little time to celebrate his victory, having to immediately march south from Yorkshire to encounter a mighty invasion force, led by Duke William, that had landed at Hastings, in East Sussex.

Harold's battle-hardened but exhausted force of Anglo-Saxon soldiers confronted the Normans on October 14 in a battle subsequently depicted on the Bayeux tapestry – a 23ft. long strip of embroidered linen thought to have been commissioned eleven years after the event by the Norman Odo of Bayeux.

Harold drew up a strong defensive position at

the top of Senlac Hill, building a shield wall to repel Duke William's cavalry and infantry.

The Normans suffered heavy losses, but through a combination of the deadly skill of their archers and the ferocious determination of their cavalry they eventually won the day.

Anglo-Saxon morale had collapsed on the battlefield as word spread through the ranks that Harold had been killed – the Bayeux Tapestry depicting this as having happened when the English king was struck by an arrow to the head.

Amidst the carnage of the battlefield, it was difficult to identify Harold – the last of the Anglo-Saxon kings.

Some sources assert William ordered his body to be thrown into the sea, while others state it was secretly buried at Waltham Abbey.

What is known with certainty, however, is that William in celebration of his great victory founded Battle Abbey, near the site of the battle, ordering that the altar be sited on the spot where Harold was believed to have fallen.

William was declared King of England on December 25, and the complete subjugation of his Anglo-Saxon subjects followed.

Those Normans who had fought on his behalf were rewarded with the lands of Anglo-Saxons, many of whom sought exile abroad as mercenaries.

Within an astonishingly short space of time, Norman manners, customs and law were imposed on England – laying the basis for what subsequently became established 'English' custom and practice.

Among those Normans granted lands by William was a family of the name of Fitz William, who settled near the village of Greatford, in what is now the South Kesteven district of Lincolnshire – and Greatford Hall became their seat.

It was in order to differentiate himself from his older brother that Arthur Fitz William changed his surname to Hall – as in Greatford Hall – in about 1090.

While the Fitz Williams and the Halls continued to flourish in Lincolnshire, branches later settled in the far north of England and also in the south of Scotland.

Some Anglo-Norman nobles, including those who later adopted the 'Hall' name, also known in Norman-French as 'de Aula', had found refuge in Scotland under King Malcom Canmore III, following an abortive rebellion against the Conqueror in 1070, while there was a further influx at the invitation of David I during his reign from 1124 to 1153.

The Halls were to be found on both sides of the border – at Redesdale in England and in Liddlesdale and East Teviotdale in Scotland.

One source has described the Halls as being feared and hated in equal measure on both sides of the border because of their fierce reputation as 'reivers.'

These reivers took their name from their lawless custom of reiving, or raiding, not only their neighbours' livestock, but also that of their neighbours across the border.

The word 'bereaved', for example, indicating to have suffered loss, derives from the original 'reived', meaning to have suffered loss of property.

A Privy Council report of 1608 graphically described how the 'wild incests, adulteries, convocation of the lieges, shooting and wearing of hackbuts, pistols, lances, daily bloodshed, oppression, and disobedience in civil matters, neither are nor has been punished.'

A constant thorn in the flesh of both the English and Scottish authorities was the cross-border raiding and pillaging carried out by well-mounted and heavily armed men, the contingent from the Scottish side of the border known and feared as 'moss troopers.'

In an attempt to bring order to what was known as the wild 'debateable land' on both sides of the border, Alexander II of Scotland had in 1237 signed the Treaty of York, which for the first time established the Scottish border with England as a line running from the Solway to the Tweed.

On either side of the border there were three 'marches' or areas of administration, the West, East and Middle Marches, and a warden governed these.

Complaints from either side of the border were dealt with on Truce Days, when the wardens of the different marches would act as arbitrators. There was also a law known as the Hot Trod, that granted anyone who had their livestock stolen the right to pursue the thieves and recover their property.

In later centuries, far from the wild borderland of old, bearers of the Hall name came to stamp their mark on the historical record of not only the British Isles but also those of other nations.

Chapter three:

Heroes and villains

Born in 1885 in Kilkenny, Frederick Hall was an Irish-Canadian recipient of the Victoria Cross (VC), the highest award for valour in the face of enemy action for British and Commonwealth forces.

Immigrating to Winnipeg in 1910, he was on the field of battle only five years later on the Western Front as a company sergeant major in the 8th (Winnipeg Rifles) Battalion, Canadian Expeditionary Forces.

In April of 1915 in Belgium, during the Second Battle of Ypres, he was posthumously awarded the VC after single-handedly rescuing a number of wounded comrades before being killed.

In 1925, Pine Street, in Winnipeg, where he had lived, was renamed Valour Road – in honour of the astonishing fact that no less than three of Canada's VC recipients during the First World War had lived on the same block of that street; the others were Leo Clarke and Robert Shankland.

One particularly intrepid bearer of the Hall

name was Virginia Hall, recognised as having been America's greatest female spy.

Born in 1906 in Baltimore, Maryland, what was to be a highly colourful and decidedly dangerous career began as a young woman when she travelled to Europe to study – later, in 1931, being appointed a consular service clerk at the U.S. Embassy in the Polish capital of Warsaw.

Her promising diplomatic career came to an abrupt end only a year later when she had to have one of her legs amputated from the knee down and replaced with a wooden appendage after she accidentally shot herself while on a hunting trip.

She travelled to Paris shortly after the start of the Second World War in 1939, joining the Ambulance Service, and later moving to Vichy – as the unoccupied area of France was known.

Then making her way to London after America's entry into the war, she volunteered for hazardous duty with Britain's Special Operations Executive (SOE), set up with the remit from Prime Minister Winston Churchill, 'to set Europe ablaze.'

Throughout the war, after being parachuted into France, she worked for both SOE and, later, its American counterpart the Office of Strategic Services

(OSS), forerunner of the CIA, playing a vital role in co-ordinating activities of the French Resistance movement.

Frustrating attempts by the Gestapo to run her to ground and known by several aliases that included *Mary of Lyon* and *Camille* – the Gestapo knew her as the elusive 'limping lady', and considered her 'the most dangerous of Allied spies.'

Six years after the end of the conflict, by which time she had married American OSS agent Paul Goillot, she joined the newly-formed CIA as an intelligence analyst.

The recipient of a number of honours and awards, including the Distinguished Service Cross, Virginia Hall died in 1982. She is the subject of a 2005 book by Judith L. Pearson, *The Wolves at the Door: The True Story of America's Greatest Female Spy*.

Taking to the heavens, Asaph Hall was the American astronomer who, in 1877, famously discovered the moons of Mars now known as Deimos and Phobos.

Born in 1829 in Goshen, Connecticut, the son of a clockmaker, he became professor of astronomy at the U.S. Naval Observatory in Washington D.C.

In addition to discovering the moons of Mars, his many other accomplishments include determining the mass of Mars and the rotation of Saturn.

Recipient in 1879 of the Gold Medal of the Royal Astronomical Society, he died in 1907, while Hall crater on the Moon and Asteroid 3299 Hall are named in his honour.

He had been married to the mathematician, abolitionist and suffragist Angeline Stickney Hall, born in 1830 in New York.

Although from an impoverished background, with the help of an older sister she was able to study mathematics, calculus, geometry and mathematical astronomy at Central College, in McGrawville, New York.

It was while at college, where she met other students of modest means, who included freed African-Americans, that she became active in the movements for the abolition of slavery and for women's rights.

She married Asaph Hall in 1856 and is thought to have helped him early in his career with his mathematical calculations while also encouraging him in his research; she died in 1892, while Stickney crater on Phobos is named for her.

Her eldest son, also named Asaph, born in

1859 and who died in 1930 followed in his father's footsteps as an astronomer and is noted for determining the mass of Saturn.

Credited with having been the first person to grow a synthetic diamond under properly verifiable and witnessed procedures, Howard Tracy Hall, better known as Tracy Hall, was the pioneering American physical chemist born in 1919 in Ogden, Utah.

It was while working in the General Electric Research Laboratory in Schenectady, New York, that he created a diamond through the synthesis and compression of carbon.

The recipient of a number of honours and awards, including the Chemical Pioneers Award from the American Institute of Chemists, he died in 2008.

Born in 1761 at Dunglass, Haddingtonshire, Sir James Hall, 4th Baronet of Dunglass, was the eminent Scottish geologist and geophysicist who wrote a number of works on the chemical composition of rock strata in addition to research on granite.

He died in 1832, while he was the father of the naval officer and early travel writer Basil Hall, born in 1788 and who died in 1844.

Educated at the Royal High School, in his native Edinburgh, he joined the Royal Navy, being commissioned as a lieutenant in 1808 and later attaining the rank of captain.

As a naval captain, he was engaged in a number of British scientific, exploration and diplomatic missions, meticulously recording all he saw in his detailed journals – a practice in which he had been encouraged by his father.

In 1817, he met with and interviewed Napoleon while the former French Emperor was living in lonely exile on the barren waste of the island of St Helena.

In the world of politics, Sir John Hall, born in 1824 in Hull, England and who later immigrated to New Zealand, served as the Independent Party Prime Minister of New Zealand from 1879 to 1882.

Interested in women's rights, it was Hall who moved the Bill in Parliament in 1893 that gave women the right to vote – the first country in the world to do so.

Also in politics, Barbara Hall, born in 1946, is the Canadian lawyer and former New Democratic Party politician who, in addition to serving as 61st Mayor of Toronto from 1994 to 1997, has also served as Chief Commissioner of the Ontario Human Rights Commission.

One particularly infamous bearer of the otherwise proud name of Hall, and one who created a media sensation when he came to trial, was the jewel thief and killer Archibald Hall, dubbed by the media "The Monster Butler" and "The Killer Butler."

Born in Glasgow in 1924, he embarked on his criminal career when he was aged 15 as a petty thief and as a burglar – but he was destined to commit decidedly more serious crimes.

Moving to London to 'fence', or sell-off, jewellery he had stolen in his native Scotland, he was apprehended and sentenced to a period of imprisonment – using his time behind bars to take elocution lessons to take the edges off his Glasgow accent and to study both antiques and the etiquette of the aristocracy.

Adopting the name Roy Fontaine on his release as homage to the actress Joan Fontaine, the bisexual Hall worked as a butler for a time before being thrown behind bars on a number of other occasions for jewellery theft.

Returning to Scotland in 1975, the smooth talking and charming Hall found employment as butler to the unsuspecting Lady Peggy Hudson in her stately home of Kirtleton House, in Dumfriesshire.

Enjoying his work and fond of his employer,

he abandoned plans to rob her of her jewellery and other precious items.

His past caught up with him in 1977 when David Wright, who had been a fellow prisoner when he had served his last prison sentence in England, found employment as a gamekeeper on the Kirtleton estate.

The pair had a furious row when Wright stole some of Lady Hudson's jewellery – a row that led to Hall shooting him dead and burying his body on the estate.

Immediately quitting his job, Hall moved back to London where he found employment as butler to Walter Scott-Elliot, an 82-year-old former MP from a wealthy aristocratic Scottish background, and his 60-year-old wife Dorothy.

Along with an accomplice, Michael Kitto, he planned to rob the couple and, unfortunately for Mrs Scott-Elliot, she walked in on them while they were discussing the plan.

Kitto responded by suffocating her, and he and Hall – with the help of the couple's housekeeper Mary Coggle – drugged Walter Scott-Elliot, bundled him and his wife's corpse into a car and drove to Scotland.

They buried Mrs Scott-Elliot in Braco, Perthshire while her husband was buried in woods near Tomich, Invernesshire after being beaten with a shovel and strangled.

Next on the murder list was Hall and Kitto's erstwhile accomplice Mary Coggle, who had taken to ostentatiously wearing some of Mrs Scott-Elliot's expensive finery, including a fur coat.

After refusing to dispose of the potentially incriminating evidence, she was beaten to death with a poker and her body dumped near a stream near Middlebie, Dumfriesshire, where it was discovered by a shepherd in December of 1977.

The next victim was Hall's half-brother Donald, whom Hall detested.

Tracking him to his holiday home in Cumbria, they tied him up, sedated him with chloroform and Hall drowned him in the bath.

Putting his body into the boot of their car, the pair then drove to Scotland and booked into a hotel in North Berwick before disposing of it – but hotel staff became suspicious of their shifty movements and called the police.

When they arrived they noticed that the car's number plate and tax disc did not match and, opening the boot, found the body of Hall's stepbrother.

Hall, after an abortive attempt at suicide, eventually revealed the locations of the bodies he had buried and he and Kitto were charged with five murders.

Kitto was sentenced to life imprisonment for three of the murders. Hall was convicted at courts in Edinburgh and London of four murders and also sentenced to life imprisonment.

The murder of Dorothy Scott-Elliot was ordered to 'lie on file'.

The Scottish court had recommended he serve a minimum of 15 years, while the English court judge handed down a recommendation that he never be released.

Until his death in Kingston Prison, Portsmouth, in September of 2002, he was the oldest person, at the age of 78, serving a whole life tariff, while three years before his death he had published his autobiography *A Perfect Gentleman*.

Chapter four:

On the world stage

A distinguished director of both theatre and film, Sir Peter Hall was born in 1930 in Bury St Edmonds, Suffolk.

The son of a stationmaster, he studied at Cambridge University, where he produced and acted in a number of productions, before founding the Royal Shakespeare Company in the early 1960s.

Director of the National Theatre from 1973 to 1988, he was knighted for his services to theatre in 1977, while in 1999 he was the recipient of a Laurence Olivier Award.

Best known for her role from 1976 to 1988 on the long-running children's television series *Sesame Street*, **Alaina Hall** was the American actress born Bernice Ruth Reed in 1946 in Springfield, Ohio; she died in 2009.

Born in 1937 in Brighton, Alabama, **Albert Hall** is the American actor whose film credits include the 1979 *Apocalypse Now* and, from 1993, *Rookie of the Year*, while **Adrian Hall** is the English actor best known for his role as the young Jeremy Potts in the 1968 *Chitty Chitty Bang Bang*.

Born in 1959 in Staines, Middlesex, his other film credits include the 1970 *The Man Who Had Power Over Women*.

Noted for her roles in a number of acclaimed British television dramas, **Esther Hall**, born in Manchester in 1970, has credits that include *Queer as Folk*, *Men Only*, *Spooks* and *Waking the Dead*, while she also has a role in the BBC daytime soap *Doctors*.

Winner of a Tony Award for Best Supporting Actress in 1950 for her role of Bloody Mary in the stage version of the musical *South Pacific*, **Juanita Hall** was the American musical theatre and film actress born in 1901 in Keyport, New Jersey. Having also reprised the role of Bloody Mary in the screen adaptation of *South Pacific*, she died in 1968.

Nominated for an Academy Award and a Golden Globe Award in 1964 for her role in the film *The Night of the Iguana*, Shirley H. Grossman was the American actress better known by her stage name of **Grayson Hall**.

Born in Philadelphia in 1922 and having also appeared from 1966 to 1971 in the Gothic television soap *Dark Shadows*, she died in 1985.

Behind the camera lens, **Conrad Hall**, born in 1926 in Papeete, Tahiti, to an American father and part-Polynesian mother, is regarded as having been one of film history's ten most influential cinematographers.

The accolade came from the International Cinematographers Guild shortly after his death in 2003.

The recipient of Academy Awards for Best Cinematography for films that include the 1969 *Butch Cassidy and the Sundance Kid* and the 2002 *Road to Perdition*, other main films in which he was involved include, from 1967, *Cool Hand Luke* and the 1973 *Electra Glide in Blue*.

He was the father of the cinematographer **Conrad Wyn Hall**, born in 1958 in Los Angeles and whose films include *Panic Room*, from 2002, and the 2005 *Two for the Money*.

Also behind the camera lens, **William Hall**, born in 1958 in Santa Barbara, California is the writer and actor who created the U.S. television series *Single Guy* and *Watching Ellie,* and who is also known as a news anchor on America's *Saturday Night Live* television show.

Nominated for an Academy Award for Best

Director for the 1941 film *Here Comes Mr Jordan*, **Alexander Hall** was the American actor and director born in 1894 in Boston.

Engaged for a time to the actress Lucille Ball before her marriage to Desi Arnaz, he died in 1968.

In the world of music, **Adelaide Hall**, born in 1901 in Brooklyn, New York was the American jazz singer and entertainer who began her stage career when she was aged 20 in the chorus line of *Shuffle Along*.

Three years after making her Broadway debut, she married a British former seaman, Bertram Hicks, who became her business manager after he opened the Big Apple nightclub in Harlem.

She began recording with Duke Ellington in 1927, producing hits that include *Creole Love* and *I Must Have That Man*, while in 1928 she was again on Broadway starring in *Blackbirds of 1928* – the most successful all-black show in Broadway's history.

She and her husband settled in Britain in 1938, and it was here that she remained until her death in 1993 – having recorded and performed with artists, in addition to Duke Ellington, who included Art Tatum, Louis Armstrong, Fats Waller and Jools Holland.

Also in the jazz genre, **Al Hall**, born in 1915 in Jacksonville, Florida and who died in 1988, was the bassist who played for artists who included Billy Hicks, Errol Garner and Benny Goodman.

In a much different musical genre, **Lynden Hall** was the singer, songwriter, arranger and record producer who won the Best Newcomer Award at the 1988 Music of Black Origins (MOBO) Awards.

Born in 1974 in Wandsworth, London, he died at the age of only 32, having released best-selling albums that include his 1997 *Medicine 4 My Pain* and the 2005 *In Between Jobs*.

Born in Edinburgh in 1936, **Robin Hall** was the Scottish folksinger who from 1960 to 1981 was a member of the popular duo Robin Hall and Jimmie MacGregor; he died in 1998.

In the creative world of the written word, **Sarah Hall**, born in 1973 in Carlisle, Cumbria, is the English novelist and poet whose *The Electric Michelangelo* was nominated for the 2004 Man Booker Prize.

Bearers of the Hall name have also excelled in the highly competitive world of sport.

A member of the Canadian basketball team at the 1976 Olympics, **Cameron Hall** is the retired player who was born in 1957 in Hamilton, Ontario, while on the golf course **Walter Hall**, born in 1947 in Winston-Salem, is the American professional golfer whose major wins include the 2001 Canada Senior Open Championship.

One particularly colourful bearer of the Hall name was Ben Hall, known as **Brave Ben Hall**, the Australian bushranger born in 1837 in Wallis Plains, Hunter Valley.

Operating mainly in New South Wales, Hall and his gang were reckoned to have carried out more than 100 robberies between 1863 and 1865 – although the majority of ordinary folk admired him as a Robin Hood figure.

He was finally shot and killed after being ambushed by police in 1865 and became the subject of ballads that include *The Ghost of Ben Hall*.

Another colourful bearer of the name was **Anthony Hall** – who claimed he was the rightful heir to the British throne.

Born in 1898 in Shropshire, he maintained he was heir through his descent from an illegitimate son of Henry VIII and the ill-fated Anne Boleyn, born before they were married.

Setting out his claim in a number of public

speeches, he also wrote a letter to King George V in 1931 – bizarrely challenging him to a duel, with the loser to be beheaded.

The monarch wisely ignored the invitation to a duel, but Hall was arrested on a number of occasions for using 'scandalous language', fined and bound over to keep the peace.

This was rather ironical, considering that Hall was actually a serving Shropshire police officer.

He died in 1947, while his story was used as the basis of John Harrison's aptly named 1999 novel *Heir Unapparent*.